A Family of Bats

Marianne Haffner and Hans-Peter B Stutz

A & C Black · London

Contents

A & C Black (Publishers) Limited
35 Bedford Row
London WC1R 4JH
This edition © 1988 A & C Black (Publishers) Limited.

Originally published in German under the title
'Fledermause – Die geheimnisvollen Flugakrobaten'
© 1988 by Kinderbuchverlag KBV Luzern AG

Acknowledgement
The publishers would like to thank Michael Chinery
for his help and advice.

A CIP catalogue record for this book is available
from the British Library.

ISBN 0-7136-3127-9

Typeset by Method Ltd, Epping, Essex
Printed in West Germany

Introducing bats

Most people think bats are creepy or frightening but they are really timid, harmless creatures. In China and Japan, bats are thought to be lucky. When you've read this book you will be able to tell your friends why there's no need to be frightened of bats.

Bats live all over the world and there are over 900 different species. They are the only mammals that can fly. Bats belong to the order *Chiroptera* – the word means 'hand flappers' because a bat's wings are fingers with skin stretched between them.

Many bats eat insects but, in tropical countries, there are species which feed on fruit or small animals such as birds, frogs, fish or mice. Blood-sucking vampire bats live only in Central and South America.

Most bats fly by night. They find their way around in the dark by making special high-pitched noises called ultra-sonic sounds. The echoes which bounce off surrounding objects tell the bats where things are. The ultra-sonic sounds which bats make are too high for us to hear.

Waking up in spring

Bats spend the cold winter months in a deep sleep called hibernation. In spring, when the weather gets warmer, they wake up and set off to hunt for food.

You may catch a glimpse of the bats at dusk as they chase insects through the air. They often appear suddenly, twist and turn with incredible speed, and then vanish into the gathering darkness.

At dawn, when it begins to get light, they crawl back into safe, sheltered hiding places in hollow trees or roofs of buildings.

The photograph shows a mouse-eared bat. They are quite rare in Britain. An adult weighs 30 grams and has a wingspan of about 40 centimetres.

Mouse-eared bats at home

By the time the sun rises, all the mouse-eared bats in this colony are back in the rafters where they live. They hang from the beam head-downwards in rows. There are so many bats it's difficult to count them all.

As the bats settle down and find a place to sleep, they make a lot of noise. Even though we can't hear the direction-finding sounds that bats make, we can hear the squeaking and chirping noises they make to each other.

Enemies

Hanging from the steep roof beams, the bats are safe from their enemies. Few cats dare to climb so high.

When we watch bats, we have to be very quiet because they are easily frightened. As fewer and fewer people own quiet lofts and barns it becomes harder for bats to find somewhere to live.

A closer look at a bat

If you watch a colony of bats, you can see that not all of them are asleep. A lot of them are staring round the loft. Bats can't see colours, but they can tell the difference between light and dark, and they can see individual shapes.

The mouse-eared bat holds firmly on to the beam with its feet. Each of its toes has a powerful claw. A bat doesn't fall off the beam when it sleeps because it has a special locking mechanism. Its feet hold on to the beam automatically.

When a bat has to do a dropping, it climbs out of the group or turns round so that it doesn't dirty itself or its neighbours. Then it has to work its way back to its place.

Keeping cool

Mammals usually keep their body temperature the same all the time. But bats are unusual because their body temperature goes up and down.

When a mouse-eared bat is flying, its body temperature is about 40 degrees Celsius. But when the bat is asleep, its body temperature cools down to the same as the air temperature. This means the bat doesn't waste energy keeping its body warm.

On sunny days, the warm air in the loft keeps the bats warm. They hang from the roof alone or in small groups.

Keeping warm

On cool days, the temperature in the roof drops very quickly and the bats go into a sort of suspended animation.

If they are disturbed by an enemy, at first they are completely helpless. It takes them a few minutes to heat up their bodies to a working temperature. Only then can they fly away and escape. This is why the bats sleep high up in the roof where enemies can't reach them.

In cooler weather, the bats move close together and help to keep each other warm. If each bat lived on its own, it would use up much more energy keeping warm.

Giving birth

Mating takes place in autumn. The male's sperm stays inside the female's body while she hibernates. It doesn't fertilize her egg until she wakes up in the spring. In June, about two months after fertilization, each female bat gives birth to one baby.

In the summer, the female mouse-eared bats gather together in a safe hiding place to give birth and raise their young.

During the birth, the mother holds on tightly to a roof beam. She makes a bag with her tail to catch the new-born baby. The baby is born feet-first. Immediately it grips hold of the roof beam. It also holds on to one of its mother's nipples and starts to drink her milk.

The new-born bat is blind and nearly naked. Its wings are still tiny and look like chubby little hands. In the photograph at the bottom of the page, you can see the baby's big thumb with its long claw.

Baby bats

At night, the mother bats fly off to hunt for insects and leave their babies behind in the loft. On the first night, the baby bats are helpless and hang from the roof without moving. In the morning they are hungry and squeak softly to themselves. When the mothers return, they suckle their babies immediately. The baby bats feed on their mother's milk for about eight weeks.

On the second night, the babies start to explore the loft and get to know the other young bats. They crawl around the roof, gripping firmly with their sharp claws.

Bats are instinctively very clean animals. Already the babies lick their wings again and again. They also spread a special liquid over their wings to keep them supple and stop them from drying out. The liquid comes from glands on the face and wings.

Growing up

The babies grow fast. During the day, there is no peace in the loft. After one week, the babies open their eyes and their fur coat begins to grow. At this stage their fur is only a thin covering: it's a bit darker than their mothers' fur.

When they aren't feeding or sleeping, the babies hang together in small groups and clean themselves thoroughly. This is called grooming. They use the claws on their back feet to comb their fur. A bat can reach every part of its body with its feet. Grooming is tiring and hungry work.

When the young bat has collected a lot of dirt on its feet, it puts its foot into its mouth and licks it clean. As it does this, the bat holds on to the roof beam with just one foot. It has to be careful not to fall, especially if it is pushed by one of its neighbours.

If its feet get very dirty, the bat spreads its toes and carefully licks each one clean. The babies may also nibble their claws to loosen the dirt. In each group of youngsters, some bats will be cleaning their fur while others will be sleeping or screaming for their mothers.

Learning to fly

After three weeks, the young mouse-eared bats are almost fully grown. During the night, they make their first timid attempts at flying.

At first the young bats can only fly in straight lines from one beam to another. But they soon learn how to twist and turn like the adults so they can explore every corner of the loft. By early morning they are exhausted and hungry.

As soon as its mother returns from hunting, each baby calls to her with its own special squeaking noises. A mother bat can recognise her own baby by the noises it makes and by its smell.

Learning to hunt

By the beginning of August, the baby is as big as its mother and can fly well. At night, it flies with its mother out of the roof to hunt for insects. The mother bat teaches her baby the way to a nearby wood where there are plenty of juicy insects to eat.

Bats know their hunting grounds very well and can fly around them without using ultra-sonic sounds to navigate in the dark. This is useful when a bat has its mouth full of food and can't make the special high-pitched noises which help it to find its way through the tre

What do mouse-eared bats eat?

Many scientists have tried to find out what mouse-eared bats eat and how they catch their food. But it's very difficult to follow the bats on their hunting trips. By examining the droppings left by the bats under their daytime resting places, scientists have managed to discover something about the bats' feeding habits.

Most of the insect remains found in the droppings come from ground beetles, like the one in the photograph below. These beetles spend most of their time on the ground and hardly ever fly. So the mouse-eared bat must snatch its food from the woodland floor. It may even search for food on the ground, rather like a shrew.

Hibernation

In the winter, the mouse-eared bats can't find enough food. So they spend the winter hibernating in a cave or other safe place. During hibernation, the bats' body temperature drops to only a few degrees Celsius and they must not be disturbed.

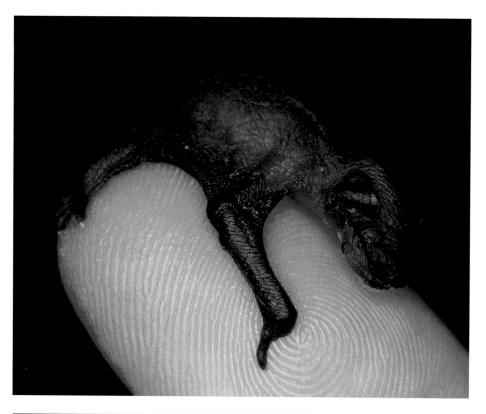

The pipistrelle

The pipistrelle is the smallest European bat. For the first few days of its life it's not much bigger than a bumblebee. Even when it's fully grown, it can just fit inside a walnut shell.

The pipistrelle weighs only six grams but can spread its wings to about 25 centimetres. Unlike the mouse-eared bat, it often gives birth to twins.

During the day, the pipistrelle hides away in holes, cracks in walls or under roof tiles. Often there's not enough space for the bat to hang by its feet, so it has to sleep on its stomach.

The pipistrelles leave tiny piles of droppings under their resting places. People don't like this dirt and often want to get rid of the bats, but they forget that the bats keep away troublesome insects.

The whiskered bat

The whiskered bat spends its day asleep in tiny gaps in barn walls. To sleep safely, it squeezes backwards into the narrowest cracks and holes. If it is frightened in its hiding place, it opens its mouth wide and wails loudly. When a predator sees the bat's sharp teeth, it usually decides to leave the bat alone.

At night, the whiskered bat catches flying insects in its sharp teeth. It hunts in parks, orchards and along hedgerows.

Long-eared bats

Long-eared bats are flying acrobats. With their wide wings they can hover in the air for several seconds. They not only catch flying insects but also snatch earwigs, spiders, caterpillars and butterflies from leaves, tree trunks and walls.

A young long-eared bat can't hold its huge ears up straight. They hang down like a spaniel's floppy ears. The youngster doesn't need to open out its ears properly until it can fly. Then it will need to use its ears to listen for flying insects.

Adult long-eared bats don't hold their ears up all the time. When an adult bat is resting, it folds back its ears and covers them with its wings. Only the little ear covers stand up.

When the bat wakes up, it bends its ears up so they look rather like horns. Just before the bat takes off, it opens out its sensitive ear trumpets. In the photograph on the right, you can see just how big the ears are.

When the long-eared bat catches a large insect, it carries the insect to a special eating place. By studying the insect remains under these eating places, scientists can work out the long-eared bat's diet.

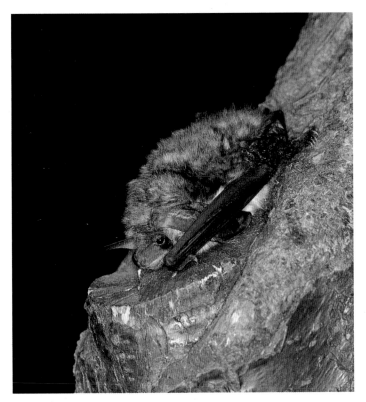

The noctule bat

The noctule bat is a fast flier and can reach speeds of up to 50 kilometres per hour. It hunts in the treetops and over water. In the photograph, you can see that a bat's wing is like a hand. The thumb stands up and has a claw on the end. The flying membrane is stretched between the long finger bones, and the back legs and tail.

Noctule bats often sleep and have their young in tree holes. Before a noctule crawls into a new hole, it sniffs the entrance carefully. The hole may already be occupied. In the mating season, the males defend their nest holes fiercely.

In the autumn, noctule bats may travel hundreds of kilometres to reach the places where they hibernate for the winter.

Save our bats

Nowadays, many bats are rare or endangered. To survive, they need a countryside with a variety of places to feed, rest and hibernate. Unfortunately, intensive farming and the growth of towns and cities makes it difficult for bats to find suitable places to live.

Scientists have managed to discover a lot about bat behaviour by using ultra-sonic detectors. With this equipment they can listen to the high-pitched sounds which the bats make. They can sometimes even tell which species of bat they are listening to. Much important information has also been gathered by observing bats in captivity.

This baby lost its mother but was reared by hand and put back into the wild. If you find a lost or injured bat, take it to a bat expert or the RSPCA.

There is still a lot we don't know about how bats move, feed and look after their young. But all the information scientists collect about the way bats live helps us to protect these fascinating creatures and make sure they survive for years to come.

Index